HOLLYWOOD

PEOPLE
AT WORK

FOR AN
AIRLINE

DEBORAH FOX

DILLON PRESS
NEW YORK

Published by Evans Brothers Limited
2a Portman Mansions
Chiltern Street
London
W1M 1LE

© 1998 Evans Brothers Limited

First published in 1998
Printed in Hong Kong by Wing King Tong

Published in the United States in 1998 by

Dillon Press
An Imprint of Macmillan Library Reference USA
A Division of Prentice-Hall, Inc.
1633 Broadway, New York, NY 10019

Commissioned by: Su Swallow
Design: Neil Sayer
Photographer: Gareth Boden
Illustrator: Liam Bonney

Acknowledgments

The author and publisher wish to thank the following for their
help: Louise Falp, Bob Noble, Pete Wenham, Captain Richard
Levy and Mary Francis of American Airlines.

We would like to thank the following for permission to
reproduce the following photographs:
American Airlines page 9, page 15 (bottom), page 19
United Airlines page 11, page 13

Library of Congress Cataloging-in-Publication Data
Fox. Deborah. 1961-
  People at work for an airline / Deborah Fox.
    p. cm. -- (People at work)
  Originally published: London: Evans Brothers, 1998.
  Includes index.
  Summary: Describes the job of a flight attendant on a
journey from London to Los Angeles and examines the work
done by a variety of other people responsible for the aircraft
and its passengers.
  1. Flight crews -- Juvenile literature.
[1. Flight crews. 2. Airlines -- Employees. 3. Occupations.]
I. Title. II. Series: Fox, Deborah, 1961- People at work.
TL547.F635 1998
387.7'3--dc21   98-28695

ISBN 0-382-42025--X (LSB)   10 9 8 7 6 5 4 3 2 1

Contents

The cabin crew

I'm Mark, and I work as a flight attendant on a Boeing 767 for a large airline. Today I am flying from London to Los Angeles, a journey of 10 hours and 24 minutes and a distance of 5,722 miles. I arrive at the airport an hour and a half before the flight. I usually check my computer to see if there are any E-mail messages for me before going to the flight briefing. This is held by the senior flight attendant. We

discuss whether we have any disabled people on board, children traveling alone, or people who need special diets.

▲ *When the cabin crew board, they check all the equipment and make sure everything needed is in place.*

Teamwork

There are ten attendants on this flight, and we all report to the senior flight attendant. The senior attendant's job is to make all the radio announcements and to make sure the cabin service goes smoothly and all the paperwork is done. Everyone on the team serves food and drinks and makes sure the passengers have everything they need.

When I finished school, I applied to join the airline. After my interviews, I was accepted, and I then went through an intensive six-week training course covering all aspects of the job–first aid, evacuation procedures, passenger service, radio training, and how to use equipment.

Preflight tests

Before every flight the aircraft is serviced by our maintenance team. They start with a "walk around" inspection to make sure there is no serious damage, such as a damaged panel or a broken windshield if a bird has hit it. Just as in a car service, technicians check the tire pressures, the brakes, and the oil levels. They also inspect the engines to make sure they are running perfectly.

◀ Tires are changed when they are worn down. This is, on average, about every 150 landings on a transatlantic journey. This mechanic checks that the landing gear is working correctly and that the tires are not damaged.

▼ It takes the aircraft fueler about 45 minutes to fill the tanks in the wings with fuel.

▲ This technician checks the oil levels in the engine.

Filling up with fuel

The fuelers fill the tanks with enough fuel to reach our destination, plus some extra in case we need to divert to another airport. Most of the fuel is stored in the wings of the aircraft so that it is equally distributed on both sides of the plane and because there is free space inside the wings. On this journey we need about 145,200 pounds of fuel, which would fill the gasoline tanks of approximately 1,400 family-sized cars.

Wheels and windshields

- A new main wheel costs about $5,000 and a nose wheel $4,500.
- There are outer and inner windshields on the aircraft.
- One windshield wiper costs about $450.
- Birds can hit the windshield as the plane takes off or lands. This is known as a "bird strike."

Check in

Children

If children need to travel alone, check-in staff arrange for someone to take them to the departure lounge. Then one of the staff members at the departure gate will make sure that the child is introduced to one of the cabin crew.

Passengers start arriving for the flight up to three hours before it is due to take off. Our check-in staff go through all the paperwork–the tickets, passports, and visas. They assign seats to passengers, deal with any special requests for seats, and label and weigh all the luggage. The weight of the luggage is recorded on our computers.

▼ People can book tickets on the telephone by calling our central reservations offices. All bookings are logged on computers, and tickets are then issued and sent out.

Through the "sniffer" machines

The luggage is sent through to special sniffer machines to make sure that it contains no explosives. The passengers themselves also go through a security check, and their carry-on luggage is sent through an X-ray machine.

▲ There are 202 people on board, so check-in agents need to work quickly.

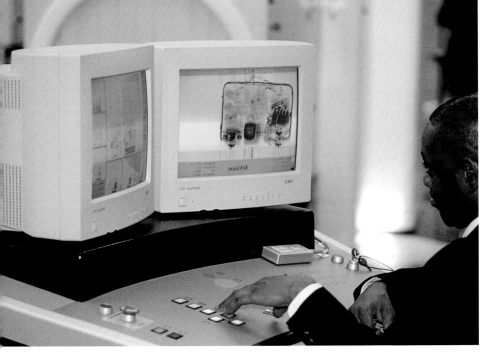

◄ Each airport has its own security staff to X-ray carry-on luggage and carry out other checks.

The flight crew arrive

It is just under an hour and a half before the flight, and the captain (pilot) and first officer (copilot) go to the operations department to pick up their flight package. This contains all the information they need for the flight—the planned route and weather details giving wind speeds, visibility, and temperatures.

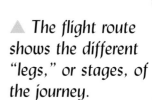

▲ The flight route shows the different "legs," or stages, of the journey.

◀ We have one flight-planning department. It creates all the flight packages and sends them to our operations teams, which are located in all the airports we use. The captain, on the left, and the first officer check through today's flight route.

The senior operations agent checks the slots and, if necessary, suggests alternative routes if we need to improve our times for takeoff.

Flight levels

- The height at which aircraft fly is called the flight level, measured in thousands of feet.
- The height at which aircraft fly is displayed on the altimeter on the flight deck.
- This aircraft will fly at a height of 37,000 feet, or 7 miles high.
- There are two tracks, or corridors, that are only for Concorde flights, and they are at a height of 10.5 miles.

"Flight plan"

All the flight plans have to be sent to a special unit in Brussels. This unit checks the flight plans and gives the airline permission to take off, allocating it a time "slot." We have requested that we wish to take off at a certain time, but it is up to the unit to confirm this.

The first officer also does a walk around inspection before the flight.

"Tracks" or "corridors"

As it flies over the Atlantic, our aircraft will follow a certain "track," or "corridor," which is really a highway in the sky. The flight planners request which tracks they want from Air Traffic Control (ATC). Each airline bids for tracks. There are up to 26, but only about 8 are used at any one time. Fewer are used when it is good, clear weather. The tracks are identified by letters of the alphabet—Track Alpha, Track Bravo, Track Charlie, Track Delta, up to Track Zebra.

Loading the aircraft

The passengers' luggage and the cargo are loaded onto the plane by the ramp services team. They work from a computer plan showing exactly how all the cargo and luggage should be positioned to keep the weight evenly distributed. This plan is known as a "load sheet." Most of the luggage and cargo are first put into containers.

▲ The ramp services team unload the bags from the dolly and transfer them to the highloader.

◀ The containers are loaded into the hold of the aircraft from the highloader.

▲ The cabin service team clean the aircraft thoroughly. They also do security checks, making sure there are no bags left on the aircraft from the previous flight.

Loading and unloading

- **dolly:** used to transport the passengers' luggage to the aircraft.
- **highloader:** larger piece of equipment with an extending bed or shelf that moves up to the hold of the aircraft. The highloader is used for loading and unloading the containers.

Although I work for a large airline, I enjoy the independence of the job. I have to be able to drive, and I really enjoy driving the larger trucks.

Nicky, cabin service agent

Cleaning

The plane is thoroughly cleaned and serviced. There are cabin service agents who work outside the aircraft, filling up the tanks for the drinking water and emptying the toilets, and agents who work inside the plane. Technicians repair any problems that we note in the log book that we keep on the plane.

Preparing for takeoff

It's half an hour before takeoff, and it is time to board. The check-in team at the departure gate make sure that everyone who is supposed to be on board is actually on board. They check all the boarding passes at the departure gate. Only when everyone is accounted for are we able to take off. As the passengers arrive, I greet them and direct them to their seats. I also help with any carry-on luggage.

Safety

It's a few minutes before takeoff, and I check that my passengers are seated and that their seat belts are fastened. Then I prepare for the safety video and indicate to the passengers where the nearest emergency exits are located.

▲ I need to make sure that all carry-on luggage is safely stored in the overhead compartments.

Before every flight we request where we would like to work on the aircraft, for example in first class or at the back of the plane.

Mary, flight attendant

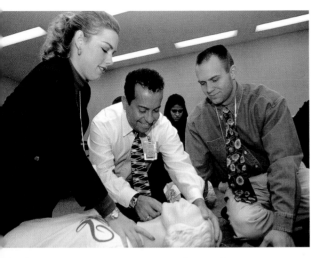

Training of cabin crew

- First aid and medical training, including giving oxygen and how to deliver a baby.
- Emergency evacuation.
- "Ditching" in the water.
- Use of life rafts and escape chutes.
- Use of smoke flares.
- Serving passengers food and drinks.
- Use of the in-flight radio system.
- Use of the in-flight entertainment system.

▲ During our training we learn how to give mouth-to-mouth resuscitation. We practice on a dummy.

▼ We also learn how to evacuate quickly if the plane has to "ditch" on water. In a swimming pool we learn how to use the life rafts.

On the flight deck

"Lights. Check. Autopilot. Check. Hydraulics. Check." The captain and first officer go through the checklist of all the essential working parts on the flight deck. On this flight there are two people who can fly the airplane –the captain and the first officer. There are three if you include the autopilot. The autopilot is a computer that can fly the plane after takeoff. In fact, it is quite possible for the autopilot to fly th whole journey itself! However, if something goes wrong with the autopilot, there are two trained people who are there to take over.
.

▼ *This pilot practices an emergency landing in a simulator, following an engine fire.*

Training of a pilot

Each airline has a requirement that all pilots must have a minimum number of flying hours. It could be 1,000 or 1,500. When they join the airline, the pilots go through an intensive training course for a month. Between 75 and 100 hours are spent on the flight simulator.

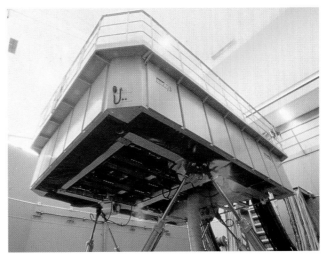

▲ *Each simulator costs several million dollars.*

"Request push back"

A vehicle called a tug pushes back the aircraft. The captain can then prepare to taxi until air traffic control gives permission for us to take off.

▼ *A ground crewman stands in front of the nose of the aircraft and indicates to the captain that it is safe to start the push back.*

Flight simulators feel just like a real aircraft—they move to simulate turbulent conditions or strong cross-winds when landing. We go through all the emergency procedures in the simulator—what to do if an engine fails, what happens if there is a fire on board, if there are electrical problems, or if the landing gear fails to come down just before landing.

Richard, captain

Help from the ground crew

When the aircraft is pushed backward, ground crewmen help the captain to avoid any obstacles. Ground crewmen walk alongside each wing carrying bright wands that the captain can see from the flight deck.

Looking after the passenger

▲ Every member of the crew has to obey the orders of the captain and follow the safety procedures.

"Cabin crew, one minute until takeoff."

With these words from the captain, we take our seats and strap ourselves in.

Food and drink

During the flight we have a strict routine. We start with serving passengers drinks before the first of their meals. The food is freshly prepared

◄ All our chefs follow rules on how meals should be prepared and served.

▲ We have special airline ovens in the galley.

and is packed in dry ice until it is loaded onto the food carts. Before serving we heat up the hot main meals in the galley, where we keep all the equipment, and then we load the trays onto the food carts.

Videos

After serving tea and coffee, one of our team changes the videotape for the next film that will be shown for two hours. During the film we serve snacks and chocolates. We collect the food trays and containers and load them

Meals
- The captain and first officer always eat different meals during the flight.
- In one month the catering group supplies over 25,000 meals for our London to Los Angeles flights.

onto the food carts. These will be put into special machines when we arrive in Los Angeles. The trays are washed, dried, and reused.

◀ We have a choice of main meals as well as special children's, vegetarian, low-fat, kosher, and seafood meals.

Keeping in touch

▼ The captain or first officer informs the flight operations and flight-planning teams of the aircraft's position throughout the flight. The teams handle hundreds of flights at any one time.

"Just letting you know we are on schedule and visibility is good," the captain radios through to our flight-planning team. Throughout the flight the captain and first officer are always open to communication. They give reports on their position to air traffic control and the flight-planning and operations teams throughout the flight.

If the airline or air traffic control need to contact the flight deck urgently and the radio is busy, they can put through a "selcal." Each aircraft has its own identity code – always four letters. When that code is entered a buzzer sounds on the flight deck. The pilots then know they need to contact base.

▲ All radio messages to the flight deck are recorded and are kept for three months.

Air traffic control

Our senoir flight attendent makes an announcement to all the passengers on the radio, "We will shortly be descending. Please return to your seats and fasten your seat belts."

"This is Flight 136 and we are ready for descent." The captain talks directly to the air traffic control tower to find out at which level we should be flying and what course we should take to the airport. Air traffic control tells the pilots which runway they should land on.

> We know everything that is going on. We see the big picture as opposed to other departments that might just see their own problem.
>
> Bob, operations manager

Landing lights

As the pilots approach the runway, they can check whether the aircraft is at the right height by the color of the landing lights on the ground.

⊙⊙⊙	the correct height
○○○	aircraft too high
●●●	aircraft too low

safe landing

For most of the journey, the captain has been flying with the autopilot. When we descend to about 3,000 feet, the captain switches off the autopilot, and the first officer takes over for the manual landing. The first officer levels the aircraft as he approaches the runway, making sure the landing gear touches the runway smoothly. As he touches down, he throttles back to slow down the aircraft.

"Please remain seated until the seat belt sign is switched off," the senior attendant tells the passengers. When the aircraft comes to a halt, we move to our positions at the exit doors to say goodbye to the passengers.

▼ All luggage is unloaded by the ground crew at Los Angeles.

▲ As soon as all the passengers have left the aircraft, I leave for a short debriefing meeting.

The takeoff is the most dynamic part of the journey, and the landing is the most critical.

Brian, first officer

▲ Our headquarters and main base are in Dallas.

Shutdown

As soon as the plane is in position and the captain and first officer have made their final checks, the captain instructs the ground crew that the power to the aircraft can be switched off. When the ground crew wish to clean and service the plane, they can switch on a separate power supply.

Debriefing

As soon as everyone has left the plane, we collect our own belongings and leave, too. After the flight all the flight attendants have a short debriefing meeting with our senior attendant to go over any problems, or to confirm that everything went well.

I have a day before my next flight back to London. One of the perks of this job is the chance I have to travel. I love visiting new places and spending time in different cities. I have put in a request to fly a new route next month, which will be exciting.

Glossary

air traffic control organization that tells pilots the height, speed, and direction at which planes must fly in a certain area to avoid a collision with another plane

autopilot short for automatic pilot; a computer that flies the plane on a pre-set course

briefing meeting held by the senior flight attendant with the cabin crew to discuss the flight and any special requests from passengers

debriefing meeting held by the senior flight attendant at the end of the flight

ditching the unlikely event of the plane having to land, or "ditch," on water

flight deck the area at the front of the plane where the captain and first officer sit. All the control instruments are on the flight deck.

hold the part of the plane where all the luggage and cargo is stored

hydraulics method of controlling the plane through liquid pressure, e.g. hydraulic brakes

landing gear the wheels of the aircraft

landing lights the lights on the runway that indicate to the pilots if they are flying too high, too low, or at the correct height

manual landing the landing of the aircraft by the pilot without the use of the autopilot

ramp services team the staff who load and unload all the luggage and cargo

selcal an emergency message to the flight deck from the operations team

shutdown when all the power to the aircraft is switched off by the pilots

sniffer machines special machines that detect bombs or explosives

throttles back to pull back the throttle; this reduces power to the engines, which slows down the plane

tug special vehicle, like a truck, that pushes back the aircraft from its parking position

turbulence gusty air currents encountered during a flight

visa document some people need giving them permission to enter another country

Index